# SELLING
## PROFESSIONALLY

# SELLING PROFESSIONALLY

Rebecca L Morgan

KOGAN
PAGE

First published in the United States of America in 1988
by Crisp Publications Inc, 95 First Street,
Los Altos, California 94022, USA

This edition first published in Great Britain in 1991
by Kogan Page Ltd, 120 Pentonville Road, London N1 9JN

Reprinted 1993

---

**British Library Cataloguing in Publication Data**

A CIP catalogue record for this book is available from the British Library.

ISBN 0–7494–0586–4

---

Typeset by DP Photosetting, Aylesbury, Bucks
Printed and bound in Great Britain by
Biddles Ltd, Guildford and King's Lynn

# Contents

# About This Book

*Selling Professionally* is not like most books. It has a unique self-paced format that encourages a reader to become personally involved. Designed to be read with a pencil in hand, it has an abundance of exercises, activities, assessments and cases that invite participation.

The object of this book is to assist anyone who is, or expects to be, a professional salesperson. It covers all aspects of selling and provides concrete suggestions and examples on how to become an efficient, effective professional salesperson.

*Selling Professionally* (and the other self-study books in this series) can be used effectively in a number of ways. Here are some possibilities:

- *Individual study.* Because the book is self-instructional, all that is needed is a quiet place, some time and a pencil. By completing the activities and exercises, the reader should not only receive valuable feedback, but also practical ideas about steps for self-improvement.

- *Workshops and seminars.* The book is ideal for assigned reading prior to a workshop or seminar. With the basics in hand, the quality of the participation should improve. More time can be spent on concept extensions and applications during the programme. The book is also effective when a trainer distributes it at the beginning of a session and leads participants through the contents.

• *Open learning*. Copies can be sent to those not able to attend head office training sessions.

There are other possibilities that depend on the objectives, programme or ideas of the user. One thing is certain; even after it has been read, this book will serve as excellent reference material which can be easily reviewed.

# Preface

Each of us is a salesperson. We have been selling our ideas, desires and opinions since we were children. Yet many professional salespeople have had little training in the nuances of sales communication.

By reading this book and completing the exercises, you will learn:

- Secrets of what makes top salespeople successful
- 37 proven methods to defrost telephone cold calls
- How to qualify your prospects
- What and what not to say in a face-to-face sales meeting
- The sales process: how to conduct the interview and get the sale
- 10 common benefits which will sell your product or service
- How to make a smooth transition from features to benefits
- A professional process for closing the sale
- How to respond positively to objections
- How to prioritise your prospects and clients.

This book provides practical, adaptable ideas which, when applied, will increase your sales immediately.

# Introduction

The sales profession can be either exhilarating or depressing. It all depends on your attitude and your ability to handle success or disappointment. When you've closed a sale it is normal to fly high. When no one is buying, dejection often occurs. This book is designed to help you do more of the former and survive the latter.

This book will assist anyone who is, or who plans to be a professional salesperson. If you are not yet in sales but considering it, first read another book in this series entitled *Sales Training Basics*.

## Sales equals service

As a professional salesperson you are actually a professional service person. To do your job properly you must be doing a service for your client. Alan Cimberg, a well-known sales trainer says, 'Stop selling and start helping.' When we sell, he explains, we are doing something *to* our prospect. When we are helping, we are doing something *for* that person.

In fact, if you are not offering a product or service which would be of use to a prospect, you are doing a disservice. If you are hesitant about suggesting a new product or a larger order because you don't want to appear too pushy, think about how your customer will feel if you have something that could help but you didn't suggest it. You both would lose.

Before you continue, answer the questions in the space provided:

What would it mean to you if you could be a better salesperson? How would your life be different?

_____

_____

_____

_____

## Sales success

### Do you have what it takes?

Sales is either an exhilarating career that adds meaning to your life or a depressing job that drives you to despair. You can enjoy a limitless income or barely scrape by. No matter what your product, company or background, much of your success is based on what *you* do.

It's easy and tempting to blame other things – the product, your boss, the company, the customer, the economy or even the weather. The truth is, however, that the ultimate factor of success or failure belongs to you.

In a US journal, Jeanne and Herbert Greenberg reported that 'more than 55 per cent of . . . [the salespeople studied] have no ability to sell. Another 25 per cent have sales ability but are selling the wrong product or service. The remaining 20 per cent are doing precisely the right jobs for themselves and their companies, and invariably they are the ones that make 80 per cent of all sales'.

We asked top sales trainers and salespeople what they thought made outstanding sales representatives.

Before you read their answers, write down as many characteristics of successful salespeople as you can think of in the space provided:

_____

_____

_____

_____

## Characteristics of successful salespeople

The attributes of successful salespeople identified by sales professionals were in four main areas: (1) commitment; (2) a healthy ego; (3) effective listening skills; and (4) humour and perspective. Of course, there is more to being a professional salesperson than these characteristics, but they are a good place to start.

### 1. Commitment

'You need to have commitment . . . real commitment to what you're doing. Total and full commitment,' comments Judy Sadlier, Senior Vice President of Dean Witter Reynolds. Judy started as a clerk in her company in 1957 and later became the first woman to complete the company's management training programme.

'A successful salesperson has persistence,' says Deanna Zimmerman, Territory Manager at Herman Miller Inc, and past president of the Association of Executive Saleswomen. 'Persistence is so important, yet most salespeople feel that after three calls to a prospect, it's time to give up. Successful professionals realise that persistence is a basic key to success. They always hang in there if the sale has potential.'

Commitment includes persistence. This means not giving up when things look bleak. Many ex-salespeople couldn't handle early failure. Either they expected instant success, or their egos were too fragile.

Pros are committed to continuous learning. Cavett Robert, a respected sales trainer and speaker says, 'School is never out for the professional.' Sheila Murray Bethel, President of Getting Control Inc, and a well-known sales speaker and trainer believes that to succeed in sales (or in life), you need to 'work harder on knowing and improving yourself than on anything else in your life'.

Tom Johnson was the number 1 Avis Leasing salesperson in the USA for three years in a row. When asked why he was so successful, he responded, 'One habit I have is to participate in one sales seminar a month, no matter how basic. If I learn one new idea from that seminar, it was worth it.'

Professional athletes continually review the basics, so why not professional salespeople?

## 2. Healthy ego

'The successful salespeople I know,' comments Pat Bailey, Regional Manager of Telos Consulting, 'use their healthy egos to measure room for improvement. They ask, "What could I have done better?"'

Top salespeople also realise a client first 'buys' them. They are confident that they can sell themselves as competent and professional.

'To be good in sales, one must understand the difference between a business refusal and a personal rejection,' offers Sheila Murray Bethel. 'Once you understand that when a client says "No" it is not a personal rejection, you make a quantum leap into the ranks of professionalism.'

Having a healthy ego also makes it easier to take calculated risks – to be bold in a positive way. Successful salespeople know they can pick themselves up and continue if their boldness causes them to fall flat.

When salespeople are proud of their company, product or service and themselves, they don't have to disparage competitors. They build upon their strengths, not the weaknesses of others.

## 3. Listening skills

A common stereotype of a salesperson is someone who talks non-stop. Actually, top sales professionals listen. Bailey explains that professional salespeople 'explore people's needs. They ask questions, and *listen*. A truly great salesperson listens, not to get information to manipulate, but to assist in serving the customer. There is no point in selling something that will cause the client "buyer's remorse". In a successful buyer/seller relationship, there is mutual interest and benefit.'

Julie Yozamp, Sales Training Manager for Digital Equipment Corporation, agrees that listening is essential for any good salesperson. 'Salespeople customers respond to are those individuals who say, "Talk to me. Tell me your problems and needs." These salespeople don't let their egos interfere. Effective questioning and listening are key skills.'

Many top salespeople see themselves as counsellors and problem-solvers. Only through effective questioning and listening can they understand the client's concerns well enough to offer solutions.

### 4. Sense of humour and enthusiasm

Judy Sadlier advises: 'You must have the ability to laugh at yourself, and avoid becoming egotistical about your successes. There have been many people who could have been more successful, but let their successes make them serious, pedantic and overbearing.'

A positive attitude is a strong asset in any profession, but especially in sales. With one, rejections become learning experiences or challenges, rather than problems. Having the perspective to learn from your mistakes helps you to develop.

Enthusiasm reflects a salesperson's excitement for the product and what it can do for the prospect. Rarely will you find a successful salesperson who isn't sincerely excited about his or her product or service.

### Summary

None of the four attributes mentioned is easy to acquire. Commitment, humour and a strong ego come easily as long as you are consistently winning. When you have days of noes, too many bad breaks and no commissions, then commitment, humour and ego may desert you. As for listening, although most of us think of ourselves as good listeners, few in fact are.

Success in sales can be yours, provided you're willing to work on these basic attributes, keep working on them, and then work some more.

Sales can drive you to the bank, or drive you crazy. Only you can decide. If you continue reading this book it's clear that your choice is to be the best professional salesperson possible.

## Professional salesperson's quiz

Be honest when taking the following quiz. We like to believe we do everything well, but unfortunately that's not always the case. See if this quiz can help you to identify some areas in need of improvement.

Scoring: 1 = Always or yes; 2 = Usually; 3 = Sometimes;
4 = Rarely; 5 = Never or no

| In sales, I am: | Always | | | Never | |
|---|---|---|---|---|---|
| 1. Assertive | 1 | 2 | 3 | 4 | 5 |
| 2. Honest | 1 | 2 | 3 | 4 | 5 |
| 3. A believer in my product | 1 | 2 | 3 | 4 | 5 |
| 4. Self-confident | 1 | 2 | 3 | 4 | 5 |
| 5. Enthusiastic | 1 | 2 | 3 | 4 | 5 |
| 6. Outgoing | 1 | 2 | 3 | 4 | 5 |
| 7. Focused on my objective | 1 | 2 | 3 | 4 | 5 |
| 8. Professional in demeanour and dress | 1 | 2 | 3 | 4 | 5 |
| 9. Displaying good posture and expression | 1 | 2 | 3 | 4 | 5 |
| 10. A good listener | 1 | 2 | 3 | 4 | 5 |
| 11. Perceptive (hear what's said as well as what isn't) | 1 | 2 | 3 | 4 | 5 |
| 12. Thinking: 'What does my prospect want?' | 1 | 2 | 3 | 4 | 5 |
| 13. Relaxed and alert | 1 | 2 | 3 | 4 | 5 |
| 14. Able to restate my prospect's needs accurately | 1 | 2 | 3 | 4 | 5 |
| 15. Anticipating concerns/objections | 1 | 2 | 3 | 4 | 5 |
| 16. Not personally rejected when someone says 'No' | 1 | 2 | 3 | 4 | 5 |
| 17. Making cold calls without any hesitation | 1 | 2 | 3 | 4 | 5 |
| 18. Prompt with follow-ups | 1 | 2 | 3 | 4 | 5 |
| 19. Generating sufficient prospects | 1 | 2 | 3 | 4 | 5 |
| 20. Willing to try new ideas | 1 | 2 | 3 | 4 | 5 |
| 21. Working smarter, not necessarily harder | 1 | 2 | 3 | 4 | 5 |
| 22. Pleasantly persistent | 1 | 2 | 3 | 4 | 5 |
| 23. Acknowledging and working on what needs improvement | 1 | 2 | 3 | 4 | 5 |
| 24. A self-starter, self-motivated | 1 | 2 | 3 | 4 | 5 |
| 25. Willing to take calculated risks | 1 | 2 | 3 | 4 | 5 |

Your score: A total of 25–50 = Excellent; 51–75 = Good;
76–100 = Need work; 101–125 = Help!

Below and opposite there is an assessment for you to copy.* Give it to your boss, a colleague, and/or selected customers – anyone who is capable of assessing your sales skills.

---

* Permission to photocopy for personal use only, not for classes or other uses.

---

## Professional salesperson's assessment

---
Salesperson's name

Thank you for taking time to help me. I am interested in your honest opinion of my skills and attitudes. Don't feel you have to 'fudge' and not tell the truth. To be the best, I need and want your candid responses.

Scoring: 1 = Always or yes; 2 = Usually; 3 = Sometimes;
4 = Rarely; 5 = Never or no

| In sales, I am usually: | Always | | | Never | |
|---|---|---|---|---|---|
| 1. Assertive | 1 | 2 | 3 | 4 | 5 |
| 2. Honest | 1 | 2 | 3 | 4 | 5 |
| 3. A believer in my product | 1 | 2 | 3 | 4 | 5 |
| 4. Self-confident | 1 | 2 | 3 | 4 | 5 |
| 5. Enthusiastic | 1 | 2 | 3 | 4 | 5 |
| 6. Outgoing | 1 | 2 | 3 | 4 | 5 |
| 7. Focused on my objective | 1 | 2 | 3 | 4 | 5 |
| 8. Professional in demeanour and dress | 1 | 2 | 3 | 4 | 5 |
| 9. Displaying good posture and expression | 1 | 2 | 3 | 4 | 5 |
| 10. A good listener | 1 | 2 | 3 | 4 | 5 |
| 11. Perceptive (hear what's said as well as what isn't) | 1 | 2 | 3 | 4 | 5 |
| 12. Thinking: 'What does my prospect want?' | 1 | 2 | 3 | 4 | 5 |
| 13. Relaxed and alert | 1 | 2 | 3 | 4 | 5 |
| 14. Able to restate my prospect's needs accurately | 1 | 2 | 3 | 4 | 5 |
| 15. Anticipating concerns/objections | 1 | 2 | 3 | 4 | 5 |
| 16. Not personally rejected when someone says 'No' | 1 | 2 | 3 | 4 | 5 |
| 17. Making cold calls without any hesitation | 1 | 2 | 3 | 4 | 5 |
| 18. Prompt with follow-ups | 1 | 2 | 3 | 4 | 5 |
| 19. Generating sufficient prospects | 1 | 2 | 3 | 4 | 5 |
| 20. Willing to try new ideas | 1 | 2 | 3 | 4 | 5 |
| 21. Working smarter, not necessarily harder | 1 | 2 | 3 | 4 | 5 |
| 22. Pleasantly persistent | 1 | 2 | 3 | 4 | 5 |
| 23. Acknowledging and working on what needs improvement | 1 | 2 | 3 | 4 | 5 |
| 24. A self-starter, self-motivated | 1 | 2 | 3 | 4 | 5 |
| 25. Willing to take calculated risks | 1 | 2 | 3 | 4 | 5 |

Your score: A total of 25–50 = Excellent; 51–75 = Good;
76–100 = Need work; 101–125 = Help!

# CHAPTER 1
# Getting Started

In Chapter 1 several key ideas will be presented including:

- Finding prospects
- Acquiring referrals
- Using the telephone to qualify and get appointments
- Overcoming telephone cold call reluctance
- Defrosting telephone cold calls
- Writing your own telephone outline
- Telephone cold call checklist

## Finding prospects

Now that you have some idea of what it takes to be a sales professional, how do you get started? To begin with, you need to identify an ample supply of prospects for your product or service.

First, realise that there are 'suspects'. These are potential clients who are not yet qualified. Also there are 'prospects': people with the need, desire and resources to buy your product or service.

Finding prospects comes from analysing suspects. Suspects and prospects can be found in many places. Some will be appropriate for what you sell and others won't. Following are several sources for you to find prospects:

### Current clients
Many salespeople forget that their best prospects are their customers. You know them and they know you. Why not begin

by offering to save them time and money with an increased order? Or perhaps, based on your knowledge of the client, an order for an additional product or service would be appropriate.

How can I use this idea? Who do I know who fits this category?

_____

_____

_____

_____

**Referrals from clients** (see page 25 on acquiring referrals)
There may be others in your clients' organisations who could use your products. Or they may have colleagues who would be ideal prospects. If you've done your job as a professional by helping your clients, following up and servicing their needs, they'll be glad to help you and others by recommending you.

Which satisfied clients can I ask for a referral?

_____

_____

_____

**Referrals from prospects who said 'No'**
Just because a prospect can't currently use (or afford) your product or service, it doesn't mean that person doesn't know someone else who can.

Who can I return to for a referral?

_____

_____

_____

**Spheres of influence**
Spheres of influence are people who can influence others with a recommendation or by lending their names as reference.

For example, if you sell stocks and shares, accountants and financial advisers would be a good sphere of influence. They could recommend your firm to their clients.

Other examples include respected members of the community or officers of professional organisations.

Who do I know who is a sphere of influence?

_____

_____

_____

**Competition**
You might not normally consider getting prospects from your competitors, but it does happen. For example, there are probably areas of your product line or service not covered by others, and vice versa. Perhaps you can agree to exchange leads.

To which competitors could I cross refer?

_____

_____

_____

**Industry association meetings and directories**
Visit your prospects' trade association meetings. Select one or two associations in which to become active. Make yourself visible, become a committee member or an officer in that organisation. Contribute to projects in which you're interested.

Secure copies of association directories for the industries to which you sell. Use these to introduce yourself to people who may be interested in your products or services.

It is usually possible to rent an association's mailing list. Using direct mail can earn you many new leads.

What associations should I join? What directories should I get?

_____

_____

_____

### Newspapers, magazines, industry periodicals

Many life insurance agents scan the marriage and birth announcements for new prospects. Others scan the business news and send clippings of promotions as a way of introduction.

How can I discover prospects by reading newspapers and magazines more effectively?

_____

_____

_____

### Yellow Pages

Some salespeople get prospects by scanning the Yellow Pages under the headings of those who use their product.

How can I find and use prospects in the Yellow Pages?

_____

_____

_____

### Friends/Acquaintances

Make sure that your friends and relatives know what you are selling. A life insurance saleswoman told her neighbours that she was a 'financial adviser' because she was too embarrassed to say 'life insurance agent'. One day she was chatting with her neighbour and he told her, 'I just bought a £100,000 life insurance policy.' Her heart sank. 'Why didn't you buy it from me?' she asked. 'I thought you were a financial adviser,' he responded. 'I didn't know you sold life insurance.'

Your friends and relatives may be able to use your product or service. If so, don't be afraid to ask, but be low key. No one likes to feel pressured into buying something.

Even if your product or service would not be applicable for friends and relatives, they may know someone who could use it.

With which friends or relatives should I discuss my product/ service?

_____

_____

_____

## Chamber of Commerce
Chambers of Commerce can be excellent sources for prospects. They often sponsor events for the sole purpose of letting members meet each other. Most publish a newsletter and/or directory. Scan these publications for prospects.

Becoming active in the committees and leadership of the Chamber can have many personal and professional benefits.

How can I get prospects through the Chamber of Commerce?

_____

_____

_____

## General directories
Some salespeople find directories such as Dun & Bradstreet's _Key British Enterprises_ or _Sell's Directory_ indispensable. Ask others in your industry if they find any directories helpful, and if so which.

How can I find out about general directories? Which ones do I know about but aren't using? How can I use them more effectively?

_____

_____

## Cold calls

Many salespeople canvass strangers by phone or in person. Some estate agents éven cold call in person in those neighbourhoods they'd like to represent. They can hit many businesses and homes in one day.

Homeowners can be leery of this approach – many of us don't like strangers coming to our door. With businesses it can be easier, especially in industries such as insurance, financial services and property agencies.

We'll cover how to make telephone cold calls later in this chapter.

How can I use cold calls? Where and who could I cold call?

_____

_____

_____


## Direct mail

Some people swear by direct mail – others swear at it. Generally, only a small percentage respond. On some mailings a 0.5 per cent return is considered good. That means for every 1000 mailers sent out, you get 5 responses. The more a list matches a prospect to your offering, the higher the response. Mailing list brokers rent lists.

How can I use direct mail? What list would I want to mail to?

_____

_____

_____

**Other ideas**

Where else can I find prospects not mentioned here? Other ideas for getting prospects:

_____

_____

_____

Try expanding your sources through one or more of the areas listed above.

## Acquiring referrals

Obtaining referrals can be difficult, especially if you're not used to asking. But once you've adopted the habit of asking, you'll receive so many that it will be hard to follow them all up.

A study conducted by a US company found that 60–80 per cent of referred leads eventually buy. And they buy an average of 23 per cent more than cold suspects. They are also four times more likely to refer you to other leads than cold prospects. It therefore clearly makes sense to ask for referrals.

Before going further, answer this question: How are you currently getting referrals?

_____

_____

_____

_____

If you've done a good job for a client, that person will be glad to suggest others you can help. But if you're not used to asking, even the phrasing of the question can be difficult. Following are some samples of what you might say:

'Tell me, George, who else do you know who might benefit from our services?'

'Maria, what other people need an improved word processor like ours?'

'Who else do you recommend I show these tax-saving ideas to?'

'By the way, Ted, before I leave, who else in your department might like to know about our special medical insurance plan?'

Have your pencil poised, ready to write down names and numbers. Some successful salespeople ask, 'If you don't mind, would you phone the prospect to say I'll be calling and tell them what we've done for you?' Or if in the same building, you might ask, 'Would you mind sparing a minute to introduce us?'

Avoid 'Do you know anyone . . .' – it is easy to say 'No'. Also, avoid telling your customer what *your* need is, ie to win a sales contest, to support your new house. Put your request in the context of helping others.

Your approach should be comfortable for you. But whatever your approach, always ask!

## Using the telephone to qualify and get appointments

Normally it is much more efficient to use a telephone to gain appointments with your sales prospects.

The good news is that the telephone will often save both time and frustration. Imagine driving 30 miles to visit a prospect only to find that she is the wrong person, not the decision-maker, or out of town. It is almost always smart to let your fingers do the walking.

The bad news is that some people are uncomfortable with telephone cold calling to gather information or make appointments. The next few pages should help.

### The importance of qualifying prospects on the phone

Why is it important to use the telephone to qualify prospects rather than making personal sales calls? Because the cost of the average personal visit has become expensive.

In what ways do you now qualify prospects before personally meeting with them?

_____

_____

_____

Analyse what you now do when using the telephone to make appointments. If you haven't been making calls but know you need to, write down what you would do.

If you don't need to make cold calls in your business, you may be tempted to skip this section. Please don't; there may be ideas that will help you in your other business conversations.

1. On the telephone I use the following techniques to get through the 'gatekeepers' (receptionists, secretaries, etc):

   _____

   _____

   _____

2. I have learned to overcome my reluctance while making telephone cold calls by:

   _____

   _____

   _____

3. Some techniques I've found useful to get appointments/make sales on the phone include:

   _____

   _____

   _____

## Overcoming telephone cold call reluctance

We all have calls we dread making. Which ones do you especially avoid?

_____

_____

_____

There are lots of reasons we avoid making these calls: we don't know what to say, we're intimidated by a person's title, we don't know who to talk to, we are afraid of coming across poorly, etc.

Some people list 'fear of the unknown', 'fear of failure' and 'fear of success' as reasons for not making cold calls. These can all be crippling fears. The best way to start confronting them is by preparing as well as you can, and then making the call.

What's the worst that can happen if you make a cold call and it doesn't go perfectly?

_____

Anything worse than that?

_____

What is the likelihood of the worst really happening?

_____

If the worst did happen, would it ruin you for ever?

_____

Normally, the worst events that could happen are 'They'll hang up' or 'They'll be condescending.' At an extreme, you may think 'I'd lose my job.' None of the 'worst' is life-threatening. This is the real bottom line. The probability of being sacked for making a cold call is next to zero. You are far more likely to get fired for _not_ making cold calls.

Isn't it worth making that call? The costs of not doing so outweigh any discomfort you may feel. Remind yourself that you have something of value to share with the person you are calling.

## Defrosting telephone cold calls

So you hate to make cold calls on the phone? Do you find yourself reading the newspaper, taking an early lunch, or even cleaning your desk to avoid making such calls? Do you tell yourself you'd make those calls if only you had some guidelines to help you know what to say? Read on for some help.

### THE PLAN

**Have a clear objective before calling**
What do you want from this call? An order? An appointment? What? The more specific your objective before the call, the more successful you will be. Write down what you want to accomplish before picking up the phone.

**Strategise before calling**
Ask yourself, 'What do I know about this prospect? Who have I/ we helped in similar industries/situations?' Make brief notes about these items so if the conversation gets off track, you'll know where to refocus it.

Call the chairman's secretary if you don't know who the best contact would be for your business.

Tell the secretary you need help. She will usually tell you who is the best person to talk to. It's a great entrée to say, 'Pat from the chairman's office said you were the person to discuss how we might increase your department's productivity.'

### THE CALL

**Start with 'Good morning/afternoon'**
This gives the person answering time to get situated and to listen to you. It is also more positive than a simple 'Hello'.

If the receptionist answers giving a name, respond by using it once in your greeting. 'Hello, John. This is Rebecca Morgan calling for Robert Anderson.'

## Give your full name and the full name of the person you're calling

Do not ask, 'Is Pat Prospect in?' or 'May I speak to Ms Prospect?' The receptionist will screen you out. Also, do not ask for the prospect by first name unless you know him or her. Don't give just your first name, either. Avoid asking for 'Mr Prospect' because that suggests you don't know Mr Prospect.

Simply say: 'Good morning/afternoon. (Your full name) calling for (prospect's full name) please.' Say it as a statement, not a question. This technique is effective because you have upset the receptionist's normal routine of 'Who's calling? From what company? What's this regarding?' You will probably find if you ask for the prospect in this way you will not be screened out most of the time.

Don't be evasive. Just answer, 'We need to discuss your widget purchasing programme.' The receptionist needs to tell your prospect *something* and as long as you're pleasant you have a good chance of being connected. Avoid 'It's personal.' This is overused, and may be resented by the prospect.

Those selling technical parts or equipment may wish to answer the receptionist's question by saying something technical like, 'It's about the 345T for the IC inside the cathode ray.' In other words, say something so technical that you are connected to the prospect without further screening.

## Be friendly to the receptionist

Ask for his or her help. Be directive rather than tentative. Pleasantly tell him or her what you need. Don't abuse these gatekeepers. They often have influencing power.

If you have trouble connecting with the prospect, ask the receptionist when you could reach him or her. He or she may even make an appointment for you to talk with the prospect on the phone.

# THE CONNECTION

### Avoid 'How are you today?' and 'You don't know me'

Both these phrases are trite and overused. They do not sound professional. If you feel you must begin your conversation explaining that you haven't met the prospect, use 'We haven't met yet.' It's more positive and sets the expectation that you will meet.

### Ask 'Are you in the middle of something urgent?'

Don't assume that because the prospect answered the phone, he isn't busy. If your prospect says, 'Yes, I am in a meeting,' ask when it would be convenient to call back. Avoid 'Do you have a minute?' 'Are you in the middle of something important?' etc. These are overused.

### Start either using a reference name or by saying, 'The purpose of my call is . . .'

'The purpose of my call is to discuss how we might be able to do business together in the area of . . .'

'_____ suggested I contact you. She thought you would be interested in how we helped her company to become more profitable.'

### Be slightly tentative

Early in the discussion, a few tentative words are usually better than definite words. Saying, 'I'm sure we could be of help to you' sounds pompous because the prospect thinks, 'How can you be so certain – you don't know anything about us?'

A strategically placed 'maybe', 'might' or 'may' shows you're willing to listen to this person's specific situation, needs and concerns. Too much uncertainty can sound as though you are unsure and incompetent. Use tentative talk judiciously and strategically.

### Verify the decision-maker

Many salespeople waste time giving a presentation to the wrong person. Verify from the beginning who the person is who makes the decision about your product/service.

'I understand you make decisions about purchasing widgets, is that correct?'

Wait for the answer. If not the right person, ask who is, then ask to be transferred to that person.

## Explain briefly how you've helped others in order to generate interest

'We have provided quality service to' (use specific industry if appropriate), 'and, I feel we may be able to serve you too.'

## Get permission before asking questions

Don't just start asking qualifying questions, ask permission first. This is so rare you will stand out as an exceptional salesperson. Ask, 'In order to see if our services may be useful, may I ask you a few brief questions?'

## Ask questions – politely

Don' talk *at* your prospect. Get him or her involved. Ideally, you should do 25 per cent of the talking and he or she the rest.

By asking the right questions you can qualify your prospect and get him or her interested in your product or service without wasting anyone's time. Some sample questions are:

'What (part/equipment/service name) are you currently using?'
'Who is (are) your current supplier(s)?'
'What do you like about your current supplier?'
(Much can be learned about the prospect by asking this question.)

'What do you look for when you consider new suppliers?'
(Find out a prospect's hot buttons when establishing a new relationship. Many people would rather stay with a medio-

cre supplier because at least the strengths and weaknesses are known. In a new supplier they hope the situation will be better, but it could also be worse. The more you know of what a prospect likes and doesn't like, the better you can determine if there is a match of his or her needs and your services.)

Most salespeople would be afraid to ask what a prospect likes about the current supplier. But much can be learned about the prospect's hot buttons by asking this question.

'What would you change about this supplier?'
(However, avoid saying, 'What don't you like about this supplier?' Many people will be too reticent to say anything bad about their current supplier because, after all, he or she made the decision to use that supplier. So the phrasing, 'What would you change about this supplier?' is deliberate to elicit information without causing defensiveness.)

'How many widgets do you purchase a month/year?'
'Who else is involved in decision-making about the purchase of widgets?'

These are, of course, sample questions. You can adapt them to your situation. Listen carefully to the prospect's tone. If your prospect sounds annoyed or impatient, you've asked too many questions. Learn to stop before this point. Start with the questions which will help you to determine if this is a suspect or prospect.

**Close for the appointment**
If all has gone well, you are ready to close for an appointment. It may be appropriate to reiterate some of the specific ways you can help your prospect, based on your discussion.

'It sounds as if our services could be of benefit to you. I'd like to meet you to find out more about your operation and discuss specifically how we could be of service to your company. Does that sound good to you?'

If you can't help, say so. Be honest.

## Avoid saying, 'I'd like to drop by.'

It suggests this appointment isn't important to you. Make the prospect feel important by setting a specific time to meet.

## Set a specific time to meet

Narrow the appointment time. Don't say, 'What time do you have available next week?' This sounds as though you have no appointments all week. Instead say: 'I'll be in your area next week. Would you rather meet Tuesday or Thursday? Morning or afternoon? Two o'clock or three?' The outdated way to do this is, 'Would Thursday at 2 or Friday at 10 be better for you?' The difference may seem slight, but the prospects will pick up on it.

Ask the prospect to write your name in his appointment book. This makes the appointment more of a commitment. Give the day *and* date because people sometimes look at the wrong week when setting appointments.

*Reconfirm the time, date and street address.* Ask for directions if you are unfamiliar with the neighbourhood.

'Good, (name of person) please put me down for Thursday, __(date)__ , at 2.00 at your office, 111 High Street. And my name again is _____ . I'm looking forward to meeting you. If something comes up, please ring me at (your phone number) and I'll do the same.'

## Be polite and courteous

Say, 'With your permission . . .', 'Thank you for your time', 'I appreciate your interest', 'If it's all right with you, may I send you some material/ask you a few questions?'

## SOME ADDITIONAL TIPS TO MAKE YOU MORE EFFECTIVE ON THE PHONE

## Deepen your voice

Deep voices are perceived as more powerful. But don't lower

your volume; if you're breathy they may wonder exactly *what* you're selling.

## Sound businesslike, but not stiff
Don't joke, but do be flexible and laugh when it is appropriate. Take your cue from the other person's tone and match it.

## Be positive and enthusiastic
Let your natural excitement about your product or service come across. Put a smile in your voice. People really can hear the difference a smile makes.

## Use the prospect's name occasionally
Calling a person by his or her name is a compliment, unless it's overdone. If used every third sentence, it sounds insincere. Be sure to use the preferred name.

## Show you're listening
Paraphrase what the prospect tells you and ask for clarification if something is unclear. Don't parrot exactly what he said. Use your own words.

While the prospect is speaking, use, 'I see', 'Uh huh', and other vocal cues to demonstrate that you're following. Any vocal acknowledgement overused can be grating, so vary your responses.

## Plan the timing of your phone calls
Decision-makers are often approachable on Mondays and Fridays, during lunch, or at the very beginning and end of a day. Often you can reach the top person directly at these times because the 'gatekeepers' are out.

## Generally, phone before sending the prospect anything
Some salespeople find it effective to write first. However, many times a prospect will not remember receiving the information. It is generally better to phone first, then send the information appropriate to what needs are discovered in the conversation. Of course, try to get an appointment before offering to send

anything. But if unsuccessful, send materials and say you'll follow up to set a time to meet and discuss it.

### At first, call a new woman prospect 'Ms' rather than Mrs, Miss, or her first name

If you haven't spoken to her before, the safest way to address her is Ms. Some women take offence at this, but most working women are used to it. If she corrects you, good. If she doesn't, ask her how she'd like to be addressed.

Sometimes you can find out the prospect's preference by asking the receptionist. But beware: this will say you don't know the prospect and you may be screened out.

### Avoid calling to confirm your first appointment with a prospect

People often cancel appointments when given the opportunity. They are suddenly 'too busy' to keep the appointment you set up with them last week.

Instead, send a 'confirmation' (not 'reminder') postcard like this:

---

Dear Ms Wilder

This is to confirm our meeting on Tuesday 15 July at 2.00 pm in your office. Please phone me if you need to retime it. I'm looking forward to meeting you.

Yours sincerely

Rebecca Morgan
120 Pentonville Road
London N1 9JN
071-278 0433

---

Have your address and phone number printed on the card. You'll be amazed at how rarely anyone alters an appointment or does not show up.

## Decide how many calls you will make if a prospect doesn't return your calls

Decide how much the potential business is worth to you. If it is worth a lot, then keep calling. Ask the receptionist when the prospect can be reached within the next few days.

## Return phone calls

If you can't personally return the call, ask someone else to contact the person for you. You never know what the call could produce.

## Always leave your name

Even though you don't expect the prospect to return your call, leave a message so that your name is familiar the next time.

## Use a minimum of 'ums', 'ahs', 'you knows' and 'yahs'

A few um's and ah's sprinkled at appropriate points can give the impression that your presentation isn't rehearsed. You can show that you aren't slick by occasionally using an 'um', 'ah', or pause. But use too many and you will be perceived as being uneducated and unintelligent, or not really listening.

## Don't read a script word for word

You may want to have prepared questions and some ideas on answering objections, but *never* read a script. You have to be an accomplished actor to avoid sounding rehearsed.

## Make it a game

Some life insurance agents celebrate the noes because statistics show that in their industry for every 24 noes there will be a 'Yes'. They tell themselves that each 'No' brings them closer to a sale.

## Tape record your side of the conversation

You can listen to yourself objectively later and make corrections.

## Say: 'I'm following up'

This is a magic phrase. When you are checking back with a prospect use 'follow up' in your initial greeting. People like others who are professional enough to follow up.

## Write your own telephone outline

1. Get through the 'gatekeeper'.
Receptionist: 'Hello. ABC Company.'
You:

_____

_____


Receptionist: 'May I tell him/her what it's regarding?'
You:

_____

_____


2. With prospect:
Prospect: 'Hello.'
You:

_____

_____

_____


What questions will you ask to spark his/her interest to meet you?

_____

_____

_____


Close the conversation and get the appointment:

_____

_____

_____

## Telephone cold call checklist

☐ I planned before picking up the phone.

☐ I thought about how I might help this prospect.

☐ I knew my response to the receptionist if she/he asked, 'What is this regarding?'

☐ I consciously deepened my voice tone.

☐ I was enthusiastic and professional.

☐ I asked qualifying questions.

☐ I avoided giving too much information.

☐ I avoided clichés.

☐ I had minimal verbal tics.

☐ If the prospect was qualified, I asked for the appointment.

### Case study

Sally has been a sales clerk in a small office supply store for a year. She has just been promoted to a new position in telephone sales. Her purpose is to call customers who haven't shopped with Speedy Office for a few months and get an appointment to explain some of Speedy's new services. Her mission is to get a sample order in the hope that they will again become regular customers.

Sally's first conversation sounded like this: 'Hello, Mr Dodd? This is uh Sally from uh Speedy Office. How is it going today? Good. Listen, you haven't been shopping with us and I want to know why. I see. Is that it? Well, maybe sometime, if it's all right with you, we could, uh, maybe meet when I'm out your way. OK? Thanks. Bye.'

How did Sally do? If you were her coach what would you recommend she do differently with her next call?

_____

_____

_____

_____

_____

See Author's response at the foot of the page.

**Author's response**

Sally is clearly unsure of herself. She needs to think about what she is going to say to the prospect and what she wants out of the conversation. It would help if she wrote some guidelines so she gets a feel for the flow of the conversation. She could also benefit from listening to an experienced salesperson to hear how that person approaches the conversation.

# CHAPTER 2
# Face-to-Face Selling

Now that sales topics such as prospecting, telephone cold calling and getting appointments have been covered, it is time to sharpen your face-to-face selling skills. This chapter will cover presentation strategies:

- Starting the interview
- Asking questions
- Facts/Features
- Benefits
- Obtaining customer feedback.

## Presentation strategies

### Preparation for face-to-face selling

Before you have a face-to-face interview with a prospect, it is important to strategise the best way to approach that person to get what you want out of your appointment.

Following are some important questions to answer before a face-to-face appointment. Of course, you will need to adjust some of the questions to fit your specific situation. A blank worksheet follows this exercise.

### Strategies for face-to-face selling

1. *What do I know about the prospect's organisation?*
   Who are their major customers?
   Who are my competitors?
   Have they changed management recently?
   How are their sales and profits?

2. *What do I know about the prospect?*
   Have I read anything about him/her?
   Have I heard about him/her from anyone else? If so, what?
   Do I know anyone who has worked with him/her?

3. *What questions do I need to ask?*
   What is the potential for use of my product/service?
   Does the organisation currently order/use my product/
   service?
   If not, why?
   If so, what do they like/dislike about using/having it?

4. *What product(s)/service(s) do I think the prospect should be interested in?*

5. *What benefits can my organisation and I provide for this prospect?*
   (These are not only benefits to the organisation, but the specific benefits for this person. This will be covered more thoroughly later in this book.)

6. *What is my objective with the appointment?*
   Arrange a demonstration? Quote for an order? Start a sample order? Introduce myself? Close a deal? The clearer you are before you walk into the interview, the more likely you are to be successful.

7. *What are the anticipated objections and how will I respond?*
   List the objection on the left and how you'll respond on the right.

| Objection | My response |
| --- | --- |
|  |  |

8. *Presentation/demonstration equipment/materials I need available*
   What do you need to bring in the way of flyers, catalogues, etc?
   Check your equipment before leaving the office to make certain it works.

9. *Similar situation examples to use*
   Who else have you been able to help in a similar situation? Be careful about using names, and don't share information that could be proprietary, sensitive or confidential.

---

You may be thinking, 'This sounds like a lot of work. Is it really worth the investment of time?'

Investment is the right word. Too few salespeople strategise before a call. Guess who does strategise? You're right – the top sales professionals.

---

## Presentation strategies worksheet

1. What do I know about the organisation?

2. What do I know about the prospect?

3. What questions do I need to ask?

4. What product(s)/service(s) do I think the prospect might need?

5. What are the benefits to this prospect?

6. What is my objective for this appointment?

7. What are the anticipated objections and how will I respond?

| Objection | My response |
|---|---|
|  |  |

8. Presentation/demonstration equipment/materials I need to have

9. Similar situation examples to be used

## Starting the interview

Before going into any sales interview, it is essential to understand the sales process. Imagine it as a funnel. At the top is the information-gathering phase. This is where most of the interview time should be. Next is the facts/benefits stage. Here is where you hone benefits to fit your prospect. Finally, the close, or agreement and commitment stage, is at the bottom of the funnel.

Many sales people focus on learning to close the sale because they have difficulty in this area. They would have much less trouble closing if they concentrated more on the earlier stages of the process.

Many people are told that the best way to start the interview is to chat about the prospect's interests. The philosophy, they say, is to establish rapport with the prospect.

Some prospects do like a small amount of socialising. However, it is easy to do too much. You may become so involved with the social topic, it will be difficult to bring the conversation round to business.

A more appropriate way to start a sales interview is to shake hands with your prospect, look him or her in the eye, have a pleasant look and be friendly, enthusiastic and businesslike. Keep the chat to a minimum. If your prospect wants to socialise, make sure your questions are geared towards what he or she wants to discuss.

Strive to make any rapport-building questions relevant to business. The questions will vary depending on what you're selling. Ask questions that will help you to understand this person and give you information to use later in the conversation.

Quickly and gracefully bring the conversation round to business and why you're there. Here's a sample:

'I'm glad we could meet today. Ms Johnson. I'm looking forward to working with you because I believe our new service might help your company to be more profitable. Let's take a look at your specific situation to see how our company might assist you.'

'Would you mind answering a few questions, so I fully understand your needs and situations?'

## Asking questions

Many salespeople start by telling the prospect about their products rather than asking questions. Why would you think it is a good idea to ask questions first?

_____

_____

You ask questions to qualify the prospect further and learn his or her hot buttons and needs.

The role of a professional salesperson is much like that of a doctor. It is necessary to diagnose the situation and prescribe a suitable treatment. Sometimes it is necessary to ask sensitive questions to determine the right prescription. Many salespeople are reluctant to do this, even after they have rapport with their prospect. Yet would you respect your doctor if you complained of lower abdominal pains and were not asked some personal questions?

### Open-ended questions

To get the most relevant information, you should ask as many open-ended questions as possible. Open-ended questions can't be answered 'Yes' or 'No' or with a simple statement of fact.

Why is it good practice to ask open-ended questions?

_____

_____

Open-ended questions encourage the prospect to talk more. Through well thought-out questions, the prospect will do most of the talking, giving you enough information to focus your comments. The answers to open-ended questions should give you insights into the prospect's feelings, values, needs and decision-making power.

Open-ended questions start with _what_, _how_, and _why_ (although 'why' can make some people defensive). Other ways to ask people to expand their comments are when you say:

Please tell me about . . .
Please explain to me . . .
Give me an idea . . .
Please describe . . .
Help me to understand . . .
Please elaborate . . .

Technically, these are not questions, but we'll consider them open-ended questions because they encourage your prospect to do the talking.

### Closed-ended questions

Closed-ended questions begin with *can, does, could, how many, how much, may, should, were, would, will, did, do, are, shall, has, have, is, was, where, when, who* and *which*. All can be answered with a 'Yes' or 'No', or simple statements of fact.

Since more information can be gathered by asking the open-ended questions, you may be thinking, 'But don't salespeople do this naturally?' Unfortunately, no. Although most salespeople know the concept, few consistently use open-ended questions.

You control the conversation when you're asking the questions. By being politely assertive, you can always bring the discussion back on target. To do this, you may have to ask some closed-ended questions such as:

'Do you have a car fleet plan?'

Make a list of the questions you normally ask in a sales interview. Then see if it makes sense to change any of your closed-ended questions into open-ended ones. To help you get started, following are questions other professionals often ask in sales interviews:

'What is the process for approving purchases?'

'What is your timetable for improving productivity?'

'If there were an ideal solution to your situation, what would it be?'

'Tell me about your widget manufacturing process.'

_____

_____

_____

Once you've gathered information from the prospect, it makes sense to focus your product or service comments on the needs you've discovered.

This seems basic, doesn't it? However, not all salespeople are astute. Some seem to ask questions because that's what they've been taught, and don't apply their product or service to this prospect's responses.

## Case study

Cynthia and Ed Browne sit down with Neal, an estate agent. Cynthia begins explaining to Neal that they recently married and want to have children soon, so they're looking for a new house. Neal interrupts her and says, 'I've got the perfect house for you. We just got some new listings and this one is beautiful. It is a cosy, one-bedroom cottage, secluded, far away from anyone, perfect for newlyweds.'

Based upon this brief interaction, do you think Neal will make a sale to the Brownes?

_____

_____

_____

_____

(See author's response at foot of page 49.)

## Facts/features, transitions and benefits

It isn't wise to sell during the information gathering stage. Save most of the information about your product or service until the facts and benefits stage. This is where you take information a prospect has given you and explain how your product or service specifically benefits him or her.

If a prospect asks, 'Tell me what you have to offer', it is all right briefly to introduce your company or product, but avoid a long monologue. You could end your response with:

'I could go on about our products and services but my comments might not touch on your specific needs. You're a busy person, so I'd like us to find out quickly if our association could be mutually beneficial. The best way to do this is for you to answer a few brief questions. All right?'

**Author's response**
Neal obviously did not listen to Cynthia's statement that they want to have children soon. Otherwise he would not have suggested a one-bedroom cottage.

Write a brief paragraph responding to a prospect who has just said, 'Tell me about what you have to offer.'

_____

_____

_____

_____

After you have an idea of your prospect's needs, tell how your product or service applies to their situation.

A transition from information gathering to features/facts and benefits might sound like this:

'Based on the information you've given me, I think we could be of service to you. The reason I say this is . . . (go into the features and benefits to this specific prospect).

### Facts/Features

The dictionary says a fact is 'a distinct or outstanding part, quality or characteristic of something'. In most sales situations, facts can be considered features.

A fact tells something that is provable. This can be about a product or company, ie how long your company has been in business, how many employees there are, how much the product weighs, etc.

List several facts/features of your company, for your products/ services:

_____

_____

_____

_____

Unfortunately, many salespeople try to _sell_ facts. People _buy_ benefits, which we will discuss shortly.

**Facts versus claims**

Be sure your facts are quantifiable. If they aren't, you are using a claim. A claim might be 'We're the best.' By what standard? Be prepared to back your statements with data. If it is an opinion, state it that way: 'Many clients feel we are the best because of our quick turnaround and low rate of rejects.'

**Transitions**

Once a feature has been stated, it should be followed with a transition. This joins a benefit to a feature. A smooth transition will always refer back to the prospect. Some samples include:

> that means for you . . .
> providing you with . . .
> what this does for you is . . .
> which means you'll benefit by . . .
> therefore you'll be able to . . .

Notice what they all have in common? 'You!'

We could say, 'this provides . . .', but saying 'this provides you' is much stronger because it helps your prospect to focus your solution on his or her situation.

**Benefits**

A benefit is 'anything contributing to an improvement in condition; to receive an advantage; a help'.

A benefit doesn't always have to follow a fact. Many successful salespeople naturally link facts and benefits, starting with a benefit to get the prospect's attention. Prospects listen better when they hear the benefit first.

Your comments need to answer the prospect's unstated question, 'So what?' When features alone are listed without being linked to benefits, many prospects think, 'What does that do for me?' This is also expressed as, 'What's in it for me?' or shortened to WIIFM. Imagine these letters emblazoned on your prospect's forehead.

A benefit clearly spells out WIIFM for the prospect. It is possible to overdo benefits. Do not oversell your prospect. Focus only on those benefits that will be of interest.

## Ten common benefits

People buy for diverse reasons. Following are ten common benefits related to buying. During fact finding it is essential to uncover which benefits are most important to your specific prospect.

The following benefits have been listed in the order in which most people buy. But each prospect and each product is different. Match your product or service with each benefit.

### 1. *To make money*

Stockbrokers help people to make money through skilful investing. Estate agents help people to make money by helping them to acquire property that will gain in value. Computer sales representatives help people to make money because of increased productivity.

How does my product/service offer profit or gain?

_____

_____

_____

### 2. *To save money*

Insurance agents help people to save money by shopping for the most protection at the best price. Industrial salespeople help customers to save money by giving quantity discounts or substituting less expensive products that still get the job done.

How does my product/service offer monetary savings?

_____

_____

_____

### 3. *To save time*

When training is included with an equipment purchase, that saves a client time. A prospect saves time when an estate agent reviews the property listings and selects only those that fit a prospect's criteria.

How does my product/service help people to save time?

_____

_____

_____

4. *For recognition*

The prospects will get recognition from their staff for buying this product to help them be more productive and make their lives easier. A local branch of a clearing bank sells recognition because of more personal service.

How does my product/service offer recognition?

_____

_____

_____

5. *For security/Peace of mind*

A prospect feels secure when he or she knows money was wisely invested, or that a computer company will be around to service the equipment. Security is eliminating the fear of loss.

How does my product/service offer security?

_____

_____

_____

6. *For convenience/comfort*

An 0800 number provides convenient access to customers. Comfort might be the quietness of a new car.

Efficiency or ease are other ways to say convenience and

comfort. A new copier makes copies faster. A new collection service means fewer trips to the post office.

How does my product/service offer convenience or comfort?

_____

_____

_____


### 7. *For flexibility*
A choice of payment schedules shows flexibility. So does a variety of models or multiple delivery times. A variety of options offers a choice.

How does my product/service offer flexibility?

_____

_____

_____


### 8. *For satisfaction/reliability/pleasure*
Knowing you have made the right decision provides satisfaction. When prospects research *Which?*, ask friends, and check references, chances are they will be satisfied with your product.

Personal satisfaction comes from self-improvement or increasing self-effectiveness. The purchase of this book addresses those benefits.

Pleasure can be purchased with a certain car, boat, skis, VCR or other recreational product.

How does my product/service offer satisfaction or pleasure?

_____

_____

_____

*9. For status*

A luxury car, personal computer, holiday home, or travelling first class are all examples of status purchases. When it is important to purchase products of a level at or above colleagues or peers, that is when a prospect is buying status. A teenager buys certain blue jeans to be like the 'crowd'.

Pride of ownership is another way to express status.

How does my product/service offer status?

_____

_____

_____

*10. For health*

Health could be the purchase of exercise equipment or a health club membership. It could be comprehensive health insurance or a medical specialist to help with a chronic problem. It could be new factory equipment which causes fewer injuries.

How does my product/service offer health?

_____

_____

_____

**Write your facts/features, transitions and benefits for your product or service**

| | |
|---|---|
| **Fact/Feature:** | We are less than a mile away . . . |
| **Transition:** | which means that you . . . |
| **Benefit:** | will save time because you won't have to travel across town as you have been doing. |

**Selling Professionally**

1. Fact/Feature: _____

   Transition: _____

   Benefit: _____

   _____

2. Fact/Feature: _____

   Transition: _____

   Benefit: _____

   _____

3. Fact/Feature: _____

   Transition: _____

   Benefit: _____

   _____

4. Fact/Feature: _____

   Transition: _____

   Benefit: _____

   _____

5. Fact/Feature: _____

   Transition: _____

   Benefit: _____

   _____

# CHAPTER 3
# Closing for Commitment

So far, so good. We have learned how to prospect, get an appointment, plan a presentation and covered the fundamentals of the beginning stages of face-to-face selling.

Now it is time to think about working towards closing the sale. In the next few pages we will cover:

- Testing for buying interest
- Sample closes
- Reducing resistance and countering concerns
- Overcoming objections
- The importance of non-verbal communication
- Reviewing your efforts.

## Testing for buying interest

A close is really a beginning. It is the start of an ongoing relationship. Even if you sell something that the prospect won't be needing again for several years (like a house), you still want to keep in touch with your buyers.

If the interview has gone well and your prospect seems interested, start closing the sale. Too many salespeople don't initiate a close. Instead they say, 'Why don't you think about it? I'll leave you this brochure. Call me when you've decided.' They leave business on the table for a competitor to take.

How do you know when to close? A good time would be when the customer asks about delivery or payment terms. You can close too early, which will annoy the prospect. The sense of when to close comes with experience.

A close is really a commitment. This may not mean actually getting a signed order, but could be a commitment for another meeting, for a demonstration, or approval to quote. Closes take many forms depending on the industry.

Salespeople are constantly looking for new ways to close. If a salesperson has done the required homework in qualifying, information gathering and addressing specific benefits to the prospect, closing should not be difficult.

## Take your prospect's buying temperature

Periodically, it is important to take a prospect's buying temperature by obtaining feedback. Here are some samples of how to do this:

'How does that fit your plans?'
'What do you think of this idea?'
'What do you like most about what you've heard?'
'How does this fit into your business and personal objectives?'
'I'd appreciate your objective opinion on this particular feature; would you tell me what you think?'
'Assuming we went ahead with this, how many would you need on the first order?'

Write phrases you plan to use to take the buying temperature of your prospects:

_____

_____

## Sample closes

Sometimes salespeople have trouble voicing the right words to initiate the close to a sale. Following are a few phrases you may wish to adapt to your situation:

'Which would you prefer, the red or blue?'
'Please sign here so we can start you on the plan without delay.'
'This is how it works. I'll need your signature today so we can send the information to the credit department and simultaneously to manufacturing. You will then receive your widget within three weeks.'
'Would you like to be invoiced on the 1st or on the 15th?'
'Should we ship this to your office or to another site?'
'I'd be delighted to order this for you today.'

After receiving a commitment from the prospect, summarise what he has agreed to, set a date for your next call, and thank the customer. Above all, don't walk out before getting some type of commitment.

### How not to choose a sample close

Eenie
Meenie
Mynie
Moe

## Reducing resistance and countering concerns

Wouldn't it be wonderful if everyone you contacted jumped at the opportunity to place a large order with you? Nice, but not very realistic.

Resistance or objections are natural. They are concerns expressed by the prospect. They are either real or a guise to get rid of you.

The worst objection you can encounter is one that is not voiced. There is an opportunity to overcome a stated objection, but you can never counter an unstated one. So be glad when a prospect shares a concern.

Some prospects bring up objections to test the salesperson. If your response is timid or not well stated, the prospect may lose respect for you and decide not to order.

There are several objections that will rarely be overcome to close the sale today. These objections are: this prospect is not the decision-maker, the prospect does not like you personally, and there is no money. Sometimes these can be smoke screens, so don't give up immediately. If you discover they are true objections, you probably won't close the sale today.

## Probe for objections
If you have tried to close a sale and the prospect says, 'I want to think about it', or 'I don't know', you need to uncover the objection(s). Ask the prospect about the hidden objection.

'What would cause you not to choose this product/service?'
'What reservations do you have?'
'Will you be frank with me? What is causing you to hesitate?'
'Do you mind my asking why you feel that way?'
'It seems that something is standing in your way of making a decision today. Is it . . . ?'

## Listen carefully
Avoid preparing your response until you have heard all the concerns. Make short notes while a prospect is talking so you won't be distracted trying to remember his comment.

## Get clarification/specifics
Make sure any concern expressed is clear to you. If you hear, 'It's too expensive', find out what that means:

'Would you tell me what "too expensive" means to you?'

## Make sure the prospect is telling you the real objection
After getting an objection, you should ask:

'Is there anything else that concerns you?'
'Is there anything else causing you to hesitate?'

## Always use verbal cushions
When a prospect voices a concern, don't counter the objection immediately. First, use a verbal cushion to show you heard the concern. Some verbal cushions are:

'I understand why you might feel that way.'
'I appreciate your concern.'
'I was concerned about that too when I first heard of it until . . .'
'Others felt that way at first.'

## Use the Three Fs technique
The 'Three Fs', *feel*, *felt*, and *found*, is a classic sales technique. It works using either the first person (I) or third person (others) like this:

'I see why you *feel* that way. (cushion)
I *felt* that way at first.
So I researched why our prices were slightly higher than XYZ and *found* we have far fewer rejects.'

'I understand how you could *feel* that way. (cushion)
Others have *felt* that way at first.
But then they *found* the long-term benefits far outweigh the initial cost.'

Avoid 'I know how you feel.' This may cause defensiveness in those who think 'You have no idea how I feel.'

## End your response with a 'temperature-taking' question
Find out if your prospect agrees with and understands your

explanation. Do this after stating several benefits, by asking a question.

'Does that make sense?'
'You want durability don't you?'
'It is important to you to have minimal rejects, isn't it?'

## Avoid arguing

Don't argue with prospects, even if they give you an objection that is untrue. Dale Carnegie said, 'The only way to get the best of an argument is to avoid it.' (By the way, this works at home too.)

Avoid beginning responses with, 'Yes, but . . .' as this discounts the others reasoning and is argumentative.

Often you will hear an objection about an area you already covered. Don't be annoyed, explain it again. No one listens to 100 per cent of a presentation. Calmly restate the information in a slightly different way. Make sure your voice doesn't sound defensive.

## Keep your answers short

When responding to a concern, keep your answers brief and to the point. Don't elaborate in excessive detail.

## Change objections into sales points

Sometimes objections can be turned into sales points. It won't work with every objection, but does with some.

For example, if you sell life insurance and your prospect says, 'I plan to buy my life insurance from my brother-in-law', you might turn that into a sales point by responding:

'Developing the right life insurance policy requires answering some very personal questions. I know I wouldn't want some of my relatives privy to that sort of information about me. Many people find an unbiased party easier to talk to about their personal values, goals and financial situation.'

## Don't take it personally

You can't always get a 'Yes' even though you answer the

objections voiced. Remember what Sheila Murray Bethel said in the Introduction, 'No' is not a personal rejection, it's a business refusal. It means the prospect may not have enough information to justify buying, or the need isn't there, or the money isn't there. It does not mean you aren't a good person.

Even the best salesperson can't overcome all objections. It's important to listen carefully, probe for the underlying objection, get clarification, and then verbally cushion your response.

**Persuasive words**
Part of successful closing is selecting persuasive words. The following words have been shown to have a positive, convincing effect on people. Mark the ones you can use effectively during your sales close.

| | |
|---|---|
| Admired | Hospitality |
| Affectionate | Hunting |
| Ambition | Independent |
| Amusement | In-the-swim |
| Appetising | Love |
| Bargain | Low-cost |
| Beauty | Maximum |
| Civic pride | Modern |
| Clean | Mother |
| Courtesy | Necessary |
| Durable | Patriotism |
| Economical | Personality |
| Efficient | Popular |
| Elegance | Progress |
| Enormous | Quality |
| Excel | Recommended |
| Expressive | Relief |
| Fun | Reputation |
| Genuine | Royalty |
| Growth | Safe |
| Guaranteed | Scientific |
| Health | Sociable |
| Home | Status |

| | |
|---|---|
| Stimulating | Time-saving |
| Stylish | Thinking |
| Successful | Unique |
| Sympathy | Up-to-date |
| Tasteful | Value |
| Tested | Youth |

Reprinted with permission from *The Hot Buttoneer* published by The Lacy Institute, Paul Micali, President, So Yarmouth, MA, USA.

---

**Overcoming objections**
Complete the following chart for your objections.

| **Following are objections I often get in a sales interview:** | **Here's how I will respond in the future:** |
|---|---|
| It's too expensive. | _____ |
| | _____ |
| | _____ |
| | _____ |
| I'm not ready to buy yet. | _____ |
| | _____ |
| | _____ |
| | _____ |
| We're locked into Brand X. | _____ |
| | _____ |
| | _____ |
| | _____ |
| (Add your own.) | _____ |
| | _____ |
| | _____ |

# The importance of non-verbal communication

Believe it or not, your body language and tone of voice speak louder than your words. When first meeting someone, our impression of them is based substantially on how they dress, move, look and sound. US research has shown that on a first meeting, our impression of someone is made up of 38 per cent vocal message (eg tone of voice), 55 per cent visual (eg body language) and only 7 per cent verbal (eg words).

Even after we know someone, we believe that person's body language even more than the words. If the words don't match other non-verbal messages, we don't believe what we are being told.

Non-verbal communication is defined as any direct communication we have other than words. Following are some examples of non-verbal communication, along with suggestions for improving yours.

The best way to see your normal non-verbal communication is to be videotaped during an actual sales presentation. If this is too frightening, a second way is to ask someone whose opinion you trust to give you honest feedback, or be videotaped in a sales call role play. It is difficult for us to recognise some personal habits.

### Eye contact
Avoid darting eyes. Don't look at the floor or ceiling during a conversation. Shifty eyes do not give a positive impression. We don't trust someone who can't look us in the eye.

Maintain direct, extended eye contact without seeming intimidating. Sales made to people who are intimidated don't stick.

Look directly at the person to whom you are speaking. This is interpreted as sincere and direct. Look your prospect in the eye, not at his or her nose, forehead, or anywhere else.

### Posture
Remember when your parents used to say, 'Stand up straight'? It does make a difference. More confidence is transmitted from someone who stands up straight instead of slouching.

Avoid tilting your head to the side. This is interpreted as

subservient or timid. (It *is* acceptable to tilt your head when listening, but not when you are speaking.)

The 'weight' of your messages will be increased if you face your client directly, stand or sit appropriately close, lean forward slightly, and hold your head erect.

## Gestures

Enthusiastic or over-weak gestures can be distracting. Don't wave your hands meaninglessly in the air. And don't cradle your head in your hands because you may appear too tired to hold your head up.

A message accented with appropriate gestures takes on added emphasis. Your gestures amplify your words by reinforcing what you are saying. A simple gesture such as raising your hand to eye level while saying, 'The price may seem high . . .' then lowering it to chest level and saying, 'but it's low compared with the value you're receiving' helps to reinforce your words.

Become aware of any physical tics, eg pen biting, moustache pulling, earring twirling, tie straightening, and/or spectacle chewing. Work to overcome these distracting habits.

## Facial expression

Smile only when you *mean* to smile. Avoid compulsive smiling. Smiles are beautiful when they are sincere. But forced smiles can be distracting and interpreted negatively.

Your expressions need to agree with the message; for example, don't laugh when the meaning is serious.

## Movement

Are you aware of your walk? Your walk tells a lot about you before you open your mouth. We make judgements about people by watching them move. You want to have a confident stride, but not distracting. Walk purposefully without looking as though you're going to run people over.

Avoid swaying back and forth or 'dancing' as you talk. This movement will interfere with your message.

## Proximity/spatial distance

How close do you sit and stand to people? Different cultures have their own rules about what is too close or too far away.

Make sure your sitting and standing distance seems comfortable to your prospect. If your prospect moves back, don't move closer.

## Professional appearance

The way you dress affects how people perceive you. The purpose of your attire is to give the impression that you are a competent professional. Put the prospect at ease, and be comfortable yourself. You can use your attire strategically. You want to look like someone your prospects would want to do business with.

Dress appropriately for your particular business and clients. For example, a banker shouldn't wear jeans and a tee shirt. Clients expect bankers to look like bankers in conservative dress.

Dress at or slightly above the level of your prospect. If you call on different types of people throughout the day you may need to be creative. Make sure your clothes are clean, pressed and in good repair, and your shoes are shined and not run down at the heels.

Check to see that your personal grooming is good – recently showered and shaved, clean hair and nails, moderate make-up, hair recently cut, etc. Check your appearance in a mirror before seeing your prospect.

Women should avoid wearing clanking jewellery, slit-, mini- or tight skirts, revealing blouses or evening-type shoes. You can still look feminine as well as businesslike.

Don't wear modified sandals (open-toe and open-heel shoes). The 'appropriate' and acceptable footwear for a professional businesswoman is a low to medium-heel and closed-toe.

Carry only a briefcase, not a handbag too. The impression is more professional and organised with only one piece. You may have to leave your handbag locked in your car, or take only your wallet in your briefcase on a lunch appointment.

# The quality of speech

## Rate of speech

We make judgements about people based on how quickly or slowly they speak. Stereotypically, someone who speaks too slowly is judged to be slow in decisions and thought. Someone who speaks too quickly is judged to be slick, or a 'fast talker'.

Learn to control your rate of speech. If a prospect speaks slowly, follow suit and slow down your delivery.

At first, pace your volume and rate to match your listener. If soft spoken, tone down your voice volume. This matching of rates creates rapport and opens the lines of communication.

## Non-words

Are you aware of which non-words (um, uh, okay, you know) you habitually use? Non-words make you sound unprofessional and uneducated.

Pauses are powerful. Don't be afraid to pause while thinking of the right word.

## Tone of voice/inflection

Avoid a low inaudible voice or statements which tail off. Also, avoid ending statements on an up-note which sounds like a question.

A whispered monotone seldom convinces anyone that you mean business, while shouting arouses defensiveness. A level, well-modulated conversational statement is convincing. Make sure your tone of voice matches your intent. Sound certain when you are certain.

# Reviewing your efforts

If you want to be a top salesperson, review each sales interview immediately. Many salespeople do this mentally, but not analytically. To bring logic and objectivity to your review, try writing your answers to the following questions. Leave a blank copy of this sheet where you'll see it immediately after each call. If possible, complete it then. Be honest.

1. What did I do well?
   — Arrived on time
   — Was appropriately dressed
   — Began interview with smile and handshake
   — Asked questions to understand the prospect's situation and concerns
   — Made a smooth transition from fact finding to features and benefits
   — Focused only on benefits relevant to prospect
   — Took prospect's temperature by asking feedback questions
   — Cushioned any objection
   — Countered concerns calmly
   — Listened well
   — Closed effectively and asked for the business.

2. What wouldn't I do again?

3. What will I do differently if in a similar situation again?

**Sales feedback**

On your next sales call, ask someone you respect to be an observer. This person may be your sales manager, another salesperson, or a friend who understands the basics of selling. Be sure you can trust whoever you ask to give you honest feedback. Always explain to the client that you will bring another person along.

Ask your observer to give you specific feedback on your presentation *after* the interview and to look at your approach and style rather than technical content.

Ask your observer to circle the number which best fits his or her impression of your behaviour in each of the areas listed below, plus any other feedback on behaviour you should sustain, expand or reduce to be more effective.

## Evaluation of sales presentation

Name _____ Date _____

|  | Excellent |  | | | Needs work |
|---|---|---|---|---|---|
|  | 5 | 4 | 3 | 2 | 1 |

*Opening the interview*
Introduction clear and pleasant?
Offer hand to prospect? Smile
confidently?
Pleasant voice tone when saying
hello?

Specific comments, observations and suggestions:

|  | Excellent |  | | | Needs work |
|---|---|---|---|---|---|
|  | 5 | 4 | 3 | 2 | 1 |

*Getting down to business*
Chat at a minimum?
Introduce the purpose of the visit/
meeting smoothly?

Specific comments, observations and suggestions:

|  | Excellent |  | | | Needs work |
|---|---|---|---|---|---|
|  | 5 | 4 | 3 | 2 | 1 |

*Fact-finding*
Prospect did most of the talking?
Open-ended questions asked?
'Selling' avoided during this stage?
Good listening behaviour
demonstrated?

Specific comments, observations and suggestions:

|  | Excellent | | Needs work | | |
|---|---|---|---|---|---|
| *Facts/Benefits* | 5 | 4 | 3 | 2 | 1 |

Smooth transition into the facts/
benefits?
Was each fact translated into a
benefit for the prospect?
Was the prospect periodically asked
for feedback?

Specific comments, observations and suggestions:

|  | Excellent | | Needs work | | |
|---|---|---|---|---|---|
| *Closing* | 5 | 4 | 3 | 2 | 1 |

Asked for a commitment?
Cushioned each objection before
responding?
Responded appropriately to
objections?
Smoked out any hidden objections?

Specific comments, observations and suggestions:

|  | Excellent | | Needs work | | |
|---|---|---|---|---|---|
| *Body language* | 5 | 4 | 3 | 2 | 1 |

Showed interest in the prospect?
Were there verbal or body language
tics?
Dressed professionally and
appropriately?
Tone enthusiastic, pleasant and
confident?

Specific comments, observations and suggestions:

|  | Excellent | | Needs work | | |
|---|---|---|---|---|---|
| OVERALL EVALUATION | 5 | 4 | 3 | 2 | 1 |

# CHAPTER 4

# Understanding Your Customer

You have learned how to prospect, how to use the telephone to get an appointment, and how to prepare for a personal sales call. Also you have been through the process of face-to-face selling. Now it is time to learn more about understanding your customer and selling to different communication styles.

## Selling to different communication styles

Have you ever entered a prospect's office for the first time and wished you knew what it would take to close the sale? One of the biggest challenges professional salespeople face is how to deal with the different personality types they encounter. Each new sales situation is unique because of the human factor. Basically, however, people can be generally categorised into four main styles. The four primary styles have various labels, described below.

The early modern work on personality classification was done by Carl Jung who labelled the four groups as: Thinkers, Sensors, Feelers and Intuitors. This book refers to the four styles as Detail Seekers, Results Seekers, Excitement Seekers and Harmony Seekers. We will explore how each of these styles needs to be approached differently in a sales situation.

Remember that although we will be using stereotypes for the purpose of illustration, rarely are people a single style. We all tend towards one style, but most of us have characteristics which can be categorised in at least one other style.

# The four communication styles

## 1. Detail Seeker

Linda is considered cold by her associates. She is analytical by nature. Typical occupations for analyticals are lawyers, engineers, computer programmers and accountants. They are detail-orientated, logical and will check for accuracy. Make sure your numbers are correct. They seek details.

Linda's handshake is quick and distant. She creates more space between you and her than most people. Her office has considerable reference material and a good deal of paper.

Criticism is Linda's biggest fear. She will check and recheck her information to verify its validity. The benefits she responds to are saving money and satisfaction. She will buy if she sees she's getting value for her money. And she must feel she will be completely satisfied with the decision.

In dealing with a Detail-Seeker you should respect the need for personal space. You won't want to be too relaxed or informal. Keep yourself businesslike. Dress professionally and conservatively.

Give a Detail-Seeker the facts, and make sure they are correct. They want as much information as possible and are in no hurry to make a decision. A decision will not be made until all the options have been compared and analysed.

Who do you know (prospects, clients, colleagues, family) who is probably a Detail Seeker?

_____

_____

_____

_____

_____

## 2. Results Seeker

Typical occupations for Results Seekers include entrepreneurs, pilots, investors, professional athletes, physicians and racing drivers. They like taking risks and are highly competitive.

They, too, have little tolerance for mistakes. They have very high ego strength, are hard-nosed, assertive and confident. They are sometimes intimidating. They are extremely time-conscious and resent anyone wasting their time.

---

Our Results Seeker, Maurice, sits behind a large desk, free of clutter. He is known for his quick decisions and risk-taking. He has a clock and phone on his desk top. His office is decorated with quality furniture. Certificates, diplomas and awards adorn his walls.

Maurice's handshake is powerful, his grasp firm. He sits behind his desk and uses it to enhance his power. He may be doing something else while he talks to you. Don't expect him to be friendly.

Maurice most fears being taken advantage of. He responds to benefits of status, recognition, saving time, making money and health. If you can weave these benefits into your presentation he will be more likely to buy.

---

When you present information to Maurice, be straightforward – don't beat about the bush. Don't chat about the weather or the family. Give him one piece of paper as a summary of what you are proposing. Be forceful, but don't challenge his authority. He likes strong people willing to take a stand but he also resents people telling him what to do. This is a difficult balance.

Who do you know (prospects, clients, colleagues, family) who fits this style's description?

_____

_____

_____

## 3. Excitement Seeker

Excitement Seekers are typically artists, advertising professionals, customer service reps, writers, corporate planners; any 'idea' people. They are founders and creators, and often turn the project over to someone else because they don't have much follow-through. They are enthusiastic, imaginative, idealistic, original, and wordy. They like to have fun and entertain people. They are often disorganised.

---

Burt, our Excitement Seeker, fears the loss of social approval. He would rarely tell you he didn't like something because he fears you may not like him any more. One benefit he is prone to buy is status, so make him feel important. The same is true of recognition. Make sure you could introduce him to a stranger if you met him on the street. Because he is so creative, he values flexibility. He hates to feel boxed in. He loves to save effort, so convenience or comfort are big motivators for him.

He is the type of person who is liked by everyone. When you meet him he walks up to you and greets you with a warm grin and a friendly handshake, sometimes a two-handed one. His clothes are often attention-getters, sometimes loud colours. His office has interesting items in it, each of which has a story that Burt will gladly tell you.

In fact, Burt is so full of stories and jokes that you may not get down to the reason for the call. You must focus Burt on the purpose of the call, yet still let him feel that you are not all business. He will buy from you if he likes you, so let him warm up to you.

---

Be friendly with Burt. You can pat him on the back, touch his arm, be enthusiastic, and be quick paced. He will like it if you have sparkle. Don't wear your pinstriped suit with Burt; try something bright.

Who do you know (prospects, clients, colleagues, family) who fits this style's description?

_____

_____

_____

_____

### 4. Harmony Seeker

These people are often entertainers, teachers, nurses, social workers or psychologists. They are loyal, caring, excellent listeners, patient and the 'counsellor' type. They are slow decision-makers so you, too, must have patience.

Our Harmony Seeker, Mary, is most interested in recognition, so be sure to acknowledge her and her activities. She also likes comfort, as is evidenced by her 'homey' desk. If your product can be related to these things, she'll probably buy.

Mary has 'cute' items on her desk – a picture of her family, a plant, tissue box and Garfield plaques. She is friendly, but won't extend her hand unless you do. Her pace is slower and she is turned off by 'fast-talking salespeople'.

Harmony Seekers are often not the decision-makers, but are influencers. She may have to check with the boss before ordering, but can influence the decision. If she feels the only time you come round is when you're selling something, she'll resent it. You need to take time to develop a relationship with her. Call her just to say 'hello'.

Be warm and likeable in your body language. Make her feel important. Offer your hand, even if she doesn't offer hers. If she is the ultimate buyer, don't turn her off by being too formal. Ask her personal questions first, about the family, her weekend, her job. Then get down to business.

Harmony Seekers fear loss of security, so you must gingerly introduce something that would rock the boat. They also fear being wrong because that would upset the harmony, or they may be exposed to flak arising from the wrong decision.

Who do you know (prospects, clients, colleagues, family) who fits this style's description?

_____

_____

_____

_____

## Understand your style

Successful salespeople can be any of the four styles. Aspects of each style are needed in difficult selling situations. You should understand your basic style and work on improving aspects of styles that can help you to adjust to various sales situations.

Remember, there are intricacies about each personality group. The more aware you are of the different communication styles, the easier it will be for you to adapt your sales presentation and make your sale.

The chart overleaf illustrates the shared characteristics among different styles. Often a person will have an overlapping characteristic of an adjoining style. For example, a person with a primary style of Results Seeker may also have some Excitement Seeker or Detail Seeker characteristics.

Try to determine your sales style by reading the following descriptions. All four styles have pros and cons. Someone from any style can be successful in professional sales. When you've read the detailed descriptions, complete the 'What did I discover about myself' exercise on page 86.

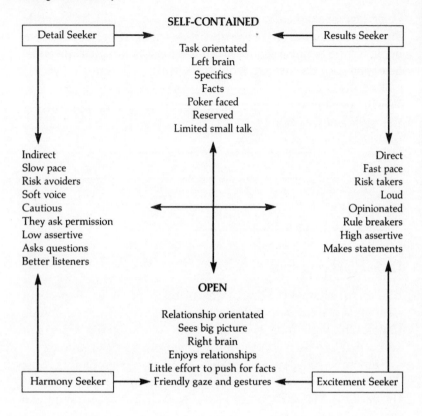

### Detail Seeker
Asks 'How?'

*Environment and body language*
Slow in speech, movements and decisions
Low voice volume
Stiff handshake
Likes personal space
Dresses conservatively, understated
Conventional surroundings
Intermittent eye contact
Limited gestures

*Characteristics*
Will ask questions about specific details
Measures your competence by how much time you spend on a
    project
Sensitive
Accurate and perfectionist
Concentrates on details
Checks for accuracy
Follows directives and standards
Likes structure
Thinks critically
Complies with authority
Cautious decision-maker, over-reliance on data collection
History is important in decision-making
Likes to be right
Fair, prudent, deliberate
Logical, rational, objective
Ordered, businesslike
Works slowly and precisely alone

*You should*
Be exacting, specific and detailed
Speak slowly
Give straight data and have proof
Present both sides of issue
Be well organised, logical and formal
Not be over-friendly
Not rush a decision
Not be domineering
Dress conservatively in dark colours

*Wants*
Security assurance
Standard operating procedure
Sheltered environment
Reassurance
No sudden changes
Personal attention

*Needs*
Precision work
Exact job description
Scheduled performance appraisals
Someone who makes quick decisions
Much information

*Least desirable characteristics*
Verbose
Indecisive
Overly cautious
Controlled and controlling
Overly serious
Rigid

*Fear*
Criticism

*Benefits*
Save money
Satisfaction

## Results Seeker
Asks 'What?' and 'When?'

*Environment and body language*
Corner office with window
Large, clean desk (untidy cupboards)
Clock on desk
Diplomas and trophies in office
Strong handshake that shows control
Fast speech and high voice volume
'Power' clothing

*Characteristics*
Makes statements
Tells others what to do
No tolerance for mistakes, feelings or advice of others

Risk taker
Highly competitive, plays to win
Accepts challenges
Substantial ego
Desires change
Hard-nosed
Uses facts to make decisions
Purposeful listener
Pragmatic, assertive and confident
Likes to be in control
Dislikes inaction
Cool and independent

*You should*
Be prepared and brief
Prepare one-page summary, but have back-up material
Be fast paced and get to the point quickly from the start
Keep things professional and businesslike
Provide two or three options and let them make the decision
Focus on bottom-line relevance
Be assertive
Talk in terms of results
Indicate a time or bottom-line urgency
Wear conservative clothing

*Wants*
Power and authority
Prestige and challenge
Wide scope of operations
Direct answers
Freedom from supervision
Many new and varied activities

*Needs*
Difficult assignments
An occasional shock
Others who research facts
To pace self and to relax more
Direct answers

*Least desirable characteristics*
Doesn't see long-range possibilities
Status-seeking
Acts first, thinks later
Lacks trust in others
Domineering
Abrupt
Rude
Impatient

*Fear*
Being taken advantage of

*Benefits*
Save time
Recognition
Status
Make money
Health

**Excitement Seeker**
Asks 'Who?'

*Environment and body language*
Same items on desk as Harmony Seeker
Warm handshake
Fast speech and high voice volume
Steady eye contact
Vibrant or unusual clothes

*Characteristics*
High risk taker
When angry becomes passive/aggressive
Founder and creator
Articulate, wordy
Enthusiastic
Likes to have fun, which is a main motivator
Likes to entertain people

Desires to help people
Often disorganised, jumps from one activity to another
Emotional and optimistic
Doesn't like effort
Fickle listener
Problem-solving orientated
Original, imaginative and idealistic
Likes involvement
Good persuasive skills
Spontaneous
Dislikes being alone
Exaggerates and generalises

*You should*
Be lively, energetic and stimulating
Present new ideas, something unique
Give incentives
Give examples and testimonials
Allow them time to talk
Be bold, not shy
Bring up new topics openly
Be entertaining
Relate your proposal to their dreams and goals
Confirm details in writing
Be clear and direct
Wear interesting clothes

*Wants*
Public recognition
Freedom of expression
Democratic relationships
Freedom from control and detail
Saved effort
Someone to implement creativity

*Needs*
Priorities and deadlines
Participatory management

Control of time
Esteem and sense of belonging

*Least desirable characteristics*
Inattentive to detail
Scattered
Jumps to conclusions
Impractical

*Fear*
Loss of social approval

*Benefits*
Status
Recognition
Flexibility
Convenience/comfort

## Harmony Seeker
Asks 'Why?'

*Environment and body language*
Has pictures of family, tissue box, plants, 'cute' items on desk
Doesn't extend hand
Has conversational tone
Informal and personalised work space
Wears comfortable clothes

*Characteristics*
Relationship maintainer
'Counsellor' or 'Mother' type
'Owns' the world's problems
Calms excited people
Doesn't like to take initiative
Loyal, caring and possessive
Likes people
Sits or stays in one place
Has patience, shows warmth

Concentrates on tasks
Excellent listener
Slow decision-maker
Dislikes interpersonal conflict

*You should*
Speak slowly
Be friendly and informal
Ask personal questions
Extend your hand
Be warm and likeable
Be non-threatening and professional
Develop trust
Give reassurance and personal guarantees whenever you can
Offer personal assistance
Be consistent
Stress your need for help
Be empathetic and understanding
Compliment their sensitivity, personal awareness
Not be over-demanding
Not allow long time lapses without personal contact
Not rush or push too hard for immediate action or change

*Wants*
Security
Status quo
Minimum work infringement on home life
Sincere appreciation
Traditional procedures

*Needs*
Validation of self-worth
Work associates of same competence
Information on how one's efforts contribute to total effort
Guidelines for accomplishing the task
Conditioning prior to change
Encouragement of creativity

*Least desirable characteristics*
Overpersonalises
Sentimental
Postponing
Subjective
Weak at goal setting and self-direction
Holds grudges

*Fear*
Loss of security
Being wrong

*Benefits*
Recognition
Comfort

## What did I discover about myself?

### Assets
Based on the information about the four communication styles, I learned I have the following assets (positive characteristics):

1.

2.

3.

4.

5.

6.

7.

**Liabilities**

Based on the same information I can improve in the following areas:

1.

2.

3.

4.

5.

6.

7.

## Communication styles practice

1. What clues suggest that a person's communication style is Detail Seeker?

    1.

    2.

    3.

    4.

    5.

2. How would you adapt your behaviour to communicate more effectively with a Detail Seeker?

    1.

2.

3.

3. What clues suggest that a person's primary communication style is Results Seeker?

    1.

    2.

    3.

    4.

    5.

4. How would you change your behaviour to communicate more effectively with a Results Seeker?

    1.

    2.

    3.

5. What clues suggest that a person's primary communication style is a Harmony Seeker?

    1.

    2.

    3.

    4.

    5.

6. How would you change your behaviour to communicate more effectively with a Harmony Seeker?

    1.

    2.

    3.

7. What clues suggest that a person's primary communication style is Excitement Seeker?

    1.

    2.

    3.

    4.

    5.

8. How would you change your behaviour to communicate more effectively with an Excitement Seeker?

    1.

    2.

    3.

## Case studies

### 1. Jane
You have been kept waiting ten minutes by Jane, your prospect. You don't know much about her except she was brief on the phone because she said she was busy. Before granting you an

appointment she wanted to know what results your product/ service had achieved for others.

Jane buzzes her secretary to show you in. As the secretary opens the door, Jane does not look up immediately. You walk into an office which has her diplomas and awards on the wall.

Jane looks up, but doesn't come around her large desk to shake your hand; she offers it over her desk. It is a firm handshake.

How will you begin this call? What will you do to adapt your communication style to hers? What strategy will you adopt to make the sale?

_____

_____

_____

_____

_____

_____

_____

## 2. Jim

Jim kept you laughing on the phone as you called him for the appointment. He responded to your serious questions humorously. He was interested in who your customers are (both companies and individuals) and who you are. He knew a few customers you mentioned and asked how they were.

He is 15 minutes late for his appointment. His secretary says he's always late. He rushes out from his office and greets you with a warm handshake and friendly smile. He continues shaking your hand as he tells you a funny story about why he's late.

His office is disorganised and comfortable. He has many interesting conversation pieces that you'd see in a home. For example, on his wall is hanging an unusual tapestry. He notices you looking at it and tells you it's from a 'quaint little shop which a charming descendent of Shakespeare runs'. He got it for 'a pittance' and now he sends everyone there.

You realise 15 minutes have gone by as he's told you this story. How will you gracefully get down to business? How will you adapt your communication style?

_____

_____

_____

_____

_____

_____

### 3. Susan

Susan sounded stiff on the phone when you were making the appointment. She asked you to bring any studies your company had done to justify the claims it makes. She said the last representative from your industry didn't have enough data and she had to keep correcting the numbers he did have.

As you enter her office, you are amazed at all the paper on and around her desk. She even has stacks on the floor.

Her handshake is stiff, formal and distant. She is dressed in a dark, conservative suit with a bow at her neck. She doesn't smile when she meets you and seems a little uneasy.

She watches you take your seat and doesn't say a word. How will you proceed? How will you adapt your communication style? What is your strategy for making the sale?

_____

_____

_____

_____

_____

_____

### 4. Bill

Bill was friendly on the phone when you made the appointment. He said, 'Come in; let's have a cup of coffee and discuss what you've got to offer.'

When you arrive, Bill's door is open and he comes out of his office to greet you. 'I was expecting you,' he said. His handshake was warm, but not strong.

His office is comfortable. There are numerous family photos as well as plants decorating his office. He is wearing a pullover and no jacket.

He asks about your background, why you got started in this business, where you'd grown up and went to school, why you'd chosen this company. Twenty minutes have gone by before you realised you haven't discussed what you've come for.

How will you turn the conversation around? How will you adapt your communication style? What is your strategy for making this sale?

_____

_____

_____

_____

_____

_____

### Author's responses

### 1. Jane

Jane is clearly a Results Seeker. Don't chat. Get down to business immediately. Her main interest is saving time and the bottom line. Be assertive. Give her several recommendations after asking a few well thought-out questions. Be strong, but don't challenge her. Don't be intimidated.

## 2. Jim

Excitement Seeker is Jim's style. Be friendly and enthusiastic with Jim. Because of his love to talk, you will have to turn the conversation round to business pleasantly. Tell him what is exciting about your product/service and how it will save him effort. Put all decisions made in writing as he probably won't remember what they were. He loves to be in the spotlight, so reinforce how your product/service will make him a hero.

## 3. Susan

Susan's style is a Detail Seeker. Be specific and exacting. Don't guess. Do your homework. Come prepared. Substantiate figures. Present both sides of the issue. However, don't give her too much material to review or you'll never get a decision from her because she'll avoid making a decision until she's reviewed all the data.

## 4. Bill

Bill is a Harmony Seeker. He hates upsetting the status quo. Take an interest in him personally. Don't be demanding. He doesn't like to make changes, so if you suggest new procedures or products, go slowly. Offer personal assurances to help him through the transition.

# CHAPTER 5
# Organise for Greater Sales

Now that you understand the sales process and have experienced recognising the four basic communication styles, it is important to make sure you are organised to take advantage of what you have learned. The next several pages will help you to prepare yourself for greater sales results.

Lack of organisation is the downfall of many salespeople. When you are good in sales you want to be selling, not completing paperwork.

Yet without good organisation even a top face-to-face salesperson will eventually fail. This person will fail because he does not follow up on promises, complete the paperwork in time or remember the details essential to the sales process.

Some common areas of frustration are: following up, taking notes, logging relevant prospect information, making use of small pieces of time, prioritising clients and prospects, and handling paperwork. Read on for some ideas.

## Prioritising your clients and prospects

How do you decide which client to call first? Do you phone the one who is the nicest? Or do you phone the person who will take the shortest time?

Many salespeople do not prioritise calls. Prospects should be prioritised by the amount of potential business they represent. The ones who represent the largest amount become 'A' prospects. Call these people first. Prospects representing the next level of volume become 'B's, and the 'it would be nice to' calls become 'C's. Divide your prospect lead cards using the A, B or C codes.

Divide call-backs this way too. Always return calls, but prioritise the order.

There is a truism that 20 per cent of your clients provide 80 per cent of your sales. Focus your efforts on the top 20 per cent. This is not to say you should forget the other 80 per cent, but call the top 20 per cent more often. (Keep in touch with those 80 per cent because you never know when one will become part of your top 20 per cent.)

## Conquering the paperwork mountain

Most salespeople abhor paperwork. Salespeople are generally better with people than with paper.

One way to reduce the amount of time you spend on paperwork is to dictate your call reports, letters, expense reports, etc, into a micro-cassette recorder. People speak four times faster than they write.

You may think, 'But I don't have anyone to transcribe the dictation?' Why not? Even if your company does not provide support for you, you can hire a student at a modest cost to come in regularly to transcribe your paperwork. Good dictation and transcription equipment is a modest investment that should pay for itself quickly through your higher productivity.

Once you have regular help, there will be other tasks your helper can do – mailing, stamping brochures, running errands, organising your files, etc.

Following are some other ideas to help you handle your paperwork:

- After sorting, handle paper only once and make a decision.
- Open your mail over your waste bin.
- Ask yourself, 'What will happen if I bin this?' If nothing, throw it out.
- Write a response in the margin of selected correspondence and return it to the originator.
- Highlight items you want to refer back to.

- Delegate items to others.
- Save up copying and do several items at once.
- Clear out your in-tray daily or each day you're in the office.
- Complete paperwork during spare time.
- Skim if it's reference material.
- Immediately throw out unsolicited junk mail.

## Follow-up made easy: a tickler/suspense file

Following up is one of the hardest skills for salespeople to master. Many have difficulty remembering to follow up with prospects who've asked them for something specific on a future date.

The easiest way to keep track of follow-ups is by using a tickler (also known as a suspense or everyday) file. This is an accordion file with slots marked 1–31 and Jan–Dec. When someone says, 'Call me back the first of next month', simply make a note including the date, name and phone number and drop it in the appropriate slot in your file.

Sometimes a task can be simply noted in your diary. But if there is a piece of paper involved (eg prospect lead form, letter), put it somewhere you can easily retrieve it – like a tickler.

Order one from your stationery supply store.

If you will be carrying your file on trips, you may want to adapt a closed-sided accordion file so your valuable papers don't fall out.

### Helpful hints for using your tickler
Buy a 1–31 January to December file.
Check your file *every* day.
Write on your daily diary 'Check tickler' for the next three weeks.
Highlight needed information before putting in the tickler.
Put the 'tickle' date in upper right-hand corner of the paper.
At the end of the month refile next month's papers in the 1–31 section.
Keep tickler on your desk.
Staple business cards and small papers to larger papers so they don't get lost.
Write 'tickler' on your diary next to meetings which correspond to items in the file.

## Salvaging scrap time

You know how valuable your sales time is. But what are a few moments of your spare time worth? If you make £50,000 a year, then 20 minutes of spare time a day is worth £2043 a year. You may be tossing £2000 a year into the time bin. But you can use this time. All it takes is planning.

Scrap time needs to be defined. It is any time that would otherwise be wasted. It includes:

— Waiting (for a client, colleague, meeting to begin, on hold, in a queue, in clients' offices)
— Travelling (in traffic, commuting, at traffic lights, while car is warming up, on trains)
— 'No brainers' (collating, opening envelopes, stamping, closing envelopes, walking, jogging, showering, watching TV).

Scrap time normally runs from one to fifteen minutes. Most people would not do anything constructive during this period. Now you can turn scrap time into productive, prime time. Using scrap time is a choice. Sometimes you will choose to listen to the radio or daydream. That's all right. Just remember, the choice is there.

Some ideas on how to use scrap time include:

● Make a quick phone call to your office, a client or prospect.
● Plan your next sales call.
● Review what you think your client needs.
● Criticise your last sales call.
● Visualise your next sales call.
● Write 'to do' or 'to call' lists.
● Complete some paperwork.
● Listen to a motivational or informational tape.
● Read an article in your field.
● Write a quick note to a client or someone you've met.
● Do relaxation exercises.
● Practise isometrics or quick physical exercises.

Many items need forethought. To listen to informational tapes while driving you will need to have them already in your car. One salesman listens to tapes while he jogs.

Carry a few postcards so you can jot down notes to people who have given you referrals. These postcards can account for thousands in commission. If you don't have the person's address with you, hold on to the note and address and post it later.

En route to a sales call, rehearse your presentation and review whatever information you have about the client. After the call, review what happened.

Take advantage of getting the most of your scrap time. You'll be amazed at the productivity it produces. Using just ten more minutes a day equals one working week per year. Although we can't create more time, we can learn to use the time we have to make more of ourselves and for ourselves.

**Make notes**
It is helpful to note several types of information when you talk to a client. Some of the most common items to note on your call report or copy of client correspondence include:

- Date of call
- What was discussed
- Date of appointment
- Date information sent
- When to follow up
- Date account opened/sale made
- Anything else relevant to this client so you won't have to ask for information again.

## Using a prospect lead form

Organise your client calls by using a pre-printed or photocopied form outlining routine questions. Following is a sample which you should change to fit your needs. Carry several with you at all times. You never know when you will get a lead.

Prospect lead                              Date _____

Name _____

Title _____

Company _____

Address _____

Phone _____

                                           OK to use
Ref by _____ _____ name

No of personnel _____

Info _____

_____

Called _____

Results _____

_____

_____

_____

Everyone is given the same amount of time each day. How you choose to use that time makes the difference between success and failure. Make some decisions about how you're currently using your time and how you would like to use it. Follow the ideas outlined in this chapter and you'll find you can accomplish much more than you thought, and with less stress.

# CHAPTER 6
# Review

You now know what it takes to be an excellent salesperson, how to secure appointments, make a sales call, adapt to different communication styles, and organise yourself for success.

You alone are responsible for your success. You can be as successful as you'd like to be, regardless of your upbringing, education, sex, age, race, religion, height or weight. You are the only one who can choose to be a success and act to obtain the skills necessary to be successful. You must decide what actions you need to take to be more effective. By adapting the ideas in this book to your style and product, you can be more successful.

But the key is action. You cannot just dream of being a top salesperson and not call on the prospects. So use this book not only as a reference, but also as a self-motivation tool to get you moving.

## What did we cover?

### Characteristics of success
We began this book by focusing on what it takes to be a top salesperson. Common attributes of good salespeople include listening skills, commitment, healthy ego, perspective and sense of humour.

### Prospecting
We then looked at how to get started by finding prospects. We went through the step-by-step process to securing appointments over the phone.

## The sales interview

Remember to start the interview in a friendly, professional way, keeping the chat to a minimum. Ask the prospect open-ended questions to understand his or her situation and uncover the hot buttons. Always couple benefits with features. Close by asking for a commitment. And cushion the objections.

## The four communication styles

Understanding the four communication styles will help you to make more sales. Results Seekers are bottom line orientated and want the information quickly. Detail Seekers want all the information, all the facts. Harmony Seekers want relationships and personal guarantees. Excitement Seekers want ease and fun.

## Organisation

Organisation is the keystone to successful salespeople. Prioritise your prospects, and keep track of when you contact them and what was discussed. Use scrap time for increased effectiveness. Use a suspense file to follow up on leads. Don't let paperwork get you down, conquer it.

By practising the ideas in each area you are sure to improve your sales skills and be on your way to becoming the best salesperson you can be. Good luck!

# Further Reading from Kogan Page

*The Best Seller*, D Forbes Ley
*Cold Calling Techniques*, Stephan Schiffman
*How to Perfect Your Selling Skills*, Pat Weymes
*Inspired Selling*, J T Auer
*Selling by Telephone*, Len Rogers
*Selling to Win: Tested Techniques for Closing the Sale*, Richard Denny
*The 25 Most Common Sales Mistakes . . . and How to Avoid Them*,
   Stephan Schiffman

**Better Management Skills**
*Delegating for Results*, Robert B Maddux
*Effective Meeting Skills: How to Make Meetings More Productive*, Marion
   E Haynes
*Effective Performance Appraisals*, Robert B Maddux*
*Effective Presentation Skills*, Steve Mandel
*The Fifty-Minute Supervisor: A Guide for the Newly Promoted*, Elwood N
   Chapman
*How to Communicate Effectively*, Bert Decker*
*How to Develop a Positive Attitude*, Elwood N Chapman*
*How to Develop Assertiveness*, Sam R Lloyd
*How to Motivate People*, Twyla Dell*
*Make Every Minute Count: How to Manage Your Time Effectively*,
   Marion E Haynes
*Managing Disagreement Constructively*, Herbert S Kindler
*Managing Organisational Change*, C Scott and D T Jaffe

*Also available on cassette

*Managing Quality Customer Service*, William B Martin
*Project Management*, Marion E Haynes
*Risk Taking*, Herbert S Kindler
*Sales Training Basics*, Elwood N Chapman
*Successful Negotiation*, Robert B Maddux
*Team Building: An Exercise in Leadership*, Robert B Maddux
*Telemarketing Basics*, Julie Freestone and Janet Brusse